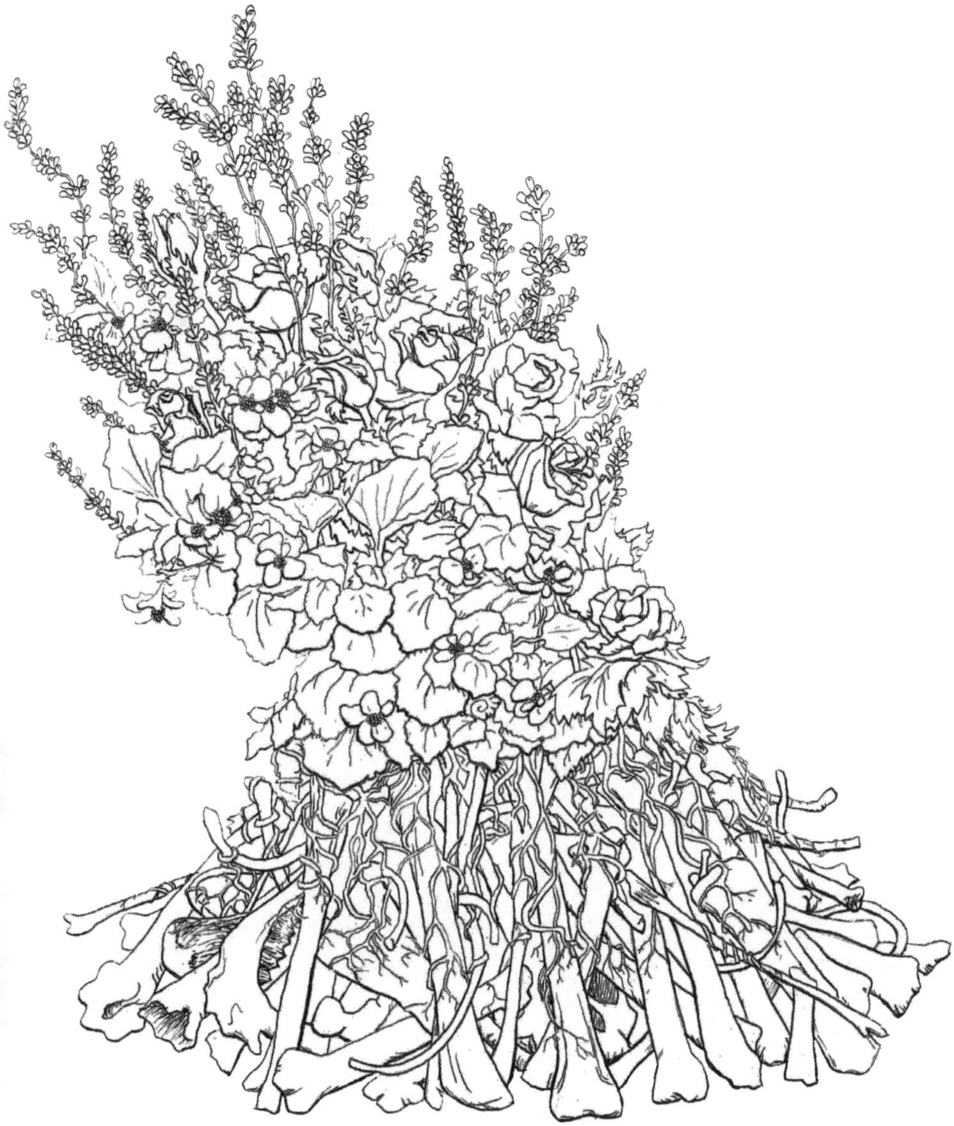

CAP

TIVE

MARTIN OTT

Winner of the 2011 De Novo Poetry Prize

CAPTIVE

Martin Ott

C&R Press / Chattanooga

Copyright © 2012 by Martin Ott

All rights reserved

Printed in the United States of America

First Edition

No part of this book may be reproduced or used in any form or by any means without written permission from the publisher. This is a work of poetry; any resemblance to actual persons or events is purely coincidental.

ISBN: 978-1-936196-10-4
LCCN: 2012933130

C&R Press
812 Westwood Ave. Suite D
Chattanooga TN 37405
www.crpress.org

Cover Art: "Fishing" by C. Buck Reynolds
Frontispiece: "Captive" by Jack Thomas Price
Book Design: John Estes

C&R Press, in partnership with Eco-Libris, plants 100 trees for each book it publishes; for more information on creating a more sustainable book culture, see www.ecolibris.net.

Acknowledgments

Thank you to the journals in which some of these poems first appeared, sometimes in a different form.

13 Miles from Cleveland / "Requiem for Pluto"
The Adirondack Review / "Shaman Gets Facelift After a Dream"
Anthology of Monterey Bay Poets, Hotel Amerika / "Syzygy"
Big Muddy / "Zen and the Art of Interrogation"
Blood Lotus / "Countdown to Harmonic Convergence"
Canteen / "The Interrogator's Fishing Tale"
Connecticut Review / "A Confused Grandmother…"
ForPoetry / "Bronzing of the Boots" & "Upon Hearing 56 Miles…"
The Greensboro Review / "Baby CPR"
Harvard Review / "Brain Bruise"
Hawai'i Review / "Dictator"
Hayden's Ferry Review / "What Has My Daughter Done Now…?"
Hotel Amerika / "Magician's Heaven"
Literary Bohemian / "Ghost Stand" & "Human Pyramid"
Many Mountains Moving / "Air Force Academy Framed by Mountains"
Margie / "Interrogator in Training"
Mudfish / "India Ivy"
Phi Kappa Phi Forum / "Norman Rockwell's 'The Mother Spanking…'"
New Letters / "Space"
New Plains Review, 3 Quarks Daily / "Interrogator's Notebook"
New Verse News / "Exchange"
Notre Dame Review / "Doors"
Poems and Plays / "Somnambulist"
Poetry East / "City of Braille"
Prairie Schooner / "The Incredible Disappearing Interrogator"
Project Verse / "The Interrogator and Priest"
Puerto del Sol / "The Alchemy of Daybreak"
Rattle / "Singing Lessons"
Raving Dove / "When Buildings Fall"
Seattle Review / "Summer Home" & "Into the White"
The Southern California Anthology / "Mapping"
Southwestern Michigan Review / "Daytrippers"
Tampa Review / "Time to a Rock"
Third Coast / "I Learned to Drive in a Cemetery"
Two Review / "Namesake"
Ucity Review / "Liar Liar"
Umbrella / "Whale Holes and Belly Buttons"
Valparaiso Poetry Review / "Breathless"
Xconnect / "Mine"

Contents

Interrogator in Training	/ 3
A Confused Grandmother Places Child Through Airport X-ray	/ 4
Syzygy	/ 5
Breathless	/ 6
Magician's Heaven	/ 7
Air Force Academy Framed by Mountains	/ 9
Line Outside Lenin's Tomb	/ 10
Baby CPR	/ 12
Interrogator's Notebook	/ 14
Shaman Gets Facelift After Dream	/ 15
What Has My Daughter Done Now to Pablo Neruda?	/ 16
The Red Button Outside Customs at the Mexico City Airport	/ 18
I Learned to Drive in a Cemetery	/ 19
Human Pyramid	/ 21
Exchange	/ 23
Mine	/ 24
Countdown to Harmonic Convergence	/ 26
Doors	/ 27
Fashion District Accessory	/ 28
Zen and the Art of Interrogation	/ 29
Space	/ 30
Liar Liar	/ 31
Time to a Rock	/ 32
The Hangman Retires in Twenty-Nine Palms	/ 34
Mapping	/ 36
The Incredible Disappearing Interrogator	/ 38
Daytrippers	/ 39
Bronzing of the Boots	/ 41

Somnambulist	/ 42
Brain Bruise	/ 43
Into the White	/ 44
The Interrogator and Priest	/ 45
Dictator	/ 46
The Moscow Metro	/ 48
Whale Holes and Belly Buttons	/ 49
Namesake	/ 50
Perishables	/ 51
Different Kinds of Fire	/ 52
Norman Rockwell's 'Mother Spanking Her Child'	/ 53
The Alchemy of Daybreak	/ 55
Captive	/ 56
The Impatient Poet	/ 57
Things I've Left Behind	/ 58
Lessons	/ 59
City of Braille	/ 61
Ghost Stand	/ 63
Requiem for Pluto	/ 64
The Lie of the Land	/ 65
When Buildings Fall	/ 66
Upon Hearing 56 Miles of the L.A. River Will Become a State Park	/ 67
The Interrogator's Fishing Tale	/ 70
India Ivy	/ 72

For India and Leo

Five mysteries hold the keys to the unseen: the act of love, and the birth of a baby, and the contemplation of great art, and being in the presence of death or disaster, and hearing the human voice lifted in song.

—Salman Rushdie
The Ground Beneath Her Feet

Interrogator in Training

The Russians were our first enemies,
but we learned all men
were equal when we plumbed
bone, fontanels and flesh.
How freeing: men could be facts,
scarves strung in fashionable nooses.
Screams from fellow interrogators
feigning torture was theater.
Our questions had barbs in them
long after we yanked in words
and occasional lips and tongues.
Can my family see the remnants
of my strange journey into manhood
practicing to snap men like bread
so we could have imaginary feasts?
When I interview job candidates
I am afraid that I will not stop
myself from the gory details of eye-
brows roasted from flaming shots,
or internal scars from fleeing dads.
Strangers still know me: I am told
more secrets than most men can hold.
Who, what, when, where, why, how:
these question words have burrowed
into me, into the marrow of me.
Now am I brave enough to ask
the most important question of all:
who am I beneath this page I hold?

A Confused Grandmother Places Child Through Airport X-ray

The plastic bin must have felt like a bassinet
to the baby, tiny feet kicking, no place to roll.
Two months out of the womb, enclosures
can seem comforting until the conveyor whirs.
Even this movement is no distress as the family
places him in the car seat and idles four cylinders
when he's too fussy to sleep. The curtain parts
and darkness blankets him. Sleepy attendants
view skull, ribs and hip bone once mistaken
for the baby's penis during ultrasound.
It is only here, with rented guards, where
the beating of a heart can be confused
with a ticking bomb and coffee overturned.
The boy's gurgle filters up to the crowd.
The belt halts. "Oh, God..." his grandmother
whimpers and the mother drops the stroller
she's been fighting to close. Time halts.
A mother's terror is not seeing her baby,
but his irradiated insides softly glowing.
His first lonely cry inside the aperture
brings her milk down and she hums
one of Beethoven's sonatas, her pregnancy
music. The X-ray beams a toothy smile.
The machine pushes him through its womb.
This time, the first to see him emerge
head first, his mother cradles him gently
in a world scared of tiny, exploding monsters.

Syzygy

The dead have lost their sense of humor.
The worms carrying jokes between tombs
have memories like sand. Roots have tickled
their ribs. They've gone to pieces. Their teeth
clatter in the wind like castanets, like cicadas.
The dead are afraid of wishbones snapped
exactly in two. They are frightened of snow
globes shattering in tiny hands. Anxious
for the girls' hemlines to plummet in fall.
The ripening of leaves with decay.
The dead have lost their sense of direction.
Up. Down. West. Atlantis. In daylight,
they trail people as shadows. At night,
they sing the refrains from show tunes
to discover their way. Whimpering. Wind.
The dead dream of butterflies that turn
into caterpillars, gorgeous and embryonic.
They daydream of snakeskin belts stolen
back by serpents. They yearn for glass
to lose its lightning and return to sand.
The dead have found me at last. A lost
grandfather. A daughter born. I see them
where before there was just rhetoric,
math and clever turns of phrase.
They smile at me reticently, knowingly.
In our glow, the dead have found their sense
of humor. Wishbones snapped in two bring
marrow and moonshine. Skulls wear caterpillars
as mustaches. Shadows of feet have bounce.
Wind and shadows rumba in candlelight.

Breathless

In basic training, we were ordered
to unmask in a tent billowing with tear
gas. I stumbled out, blinded, puking
in ferns yellow from this practice, certain
I was dying. The lesson was: masks work.
To build truth with pain. On the news,
I see men don chemical suits and dive
into bunkers, sweat coating their eye
pieces, breathless from the sprint, heat
and bomb bursts. We have always feared
the alchemist who poisons, transforms
water and air with a demon we cannot
parry. Those who dip arrows also shake
from the prick, shifting winds, enemies
torched in Hiroshima and Nagasaki.
When it is time to take off masks
the lowest ranking soldier tests the air.

Magician's Heaven

"The only way to get in the false gates
is to die onstage," Impossible O'Donnell
told his son moments before he entered
the tank for his signature trick: Water
Slaughter. At two minutes under,
the murmuring crowd was a leviathan
hissing venom into his throbbing lobes.
At three minutes, lungs are bladders
filled with razors sinking in the groin.
At four minutes, water is a mirage,
madness, a mirror. The son knew this
when he followed in his father's leg
irons across the ocean floor to a South
Pacific beach, where Viking castaways
confused him for their god Odin.
In his magician's hat, the new Impossible
O'Donnell kept his family's tricks—
the bendable bracelets, false bottom
coffins and meteoric flames bedazzling
his hosts in a longitude kept secret
by its absence, a latitude of monsoon,
eye of calm in the keyhole of handcuffs.
At five minutes under the box of water,
the son saw three generations of Impossible
O'Donnells cheating each other at cards
inside the walls of Magician's Heaven,
while Houdini and Moses smoked
cigars that coughed out snakes of ash.

At six minutes, the rescuers' axes smashed the tank, quenching the angry crowd's heat and heaving the blue son to flop onstage like a mud-dog. In the crowd, his mother searched calmly for potential wives to carry his magician's seed, and up on the ceiling, The Impossible O'Donnell watched a white pigeon from his sleeve staring down at him.

Air Force Academy Framed by Mountains

A giant bomber guards the gates
in a stand of shivering pines.
From the overpass, the entrance
to aerial superiority is clouded.
Killing from a great height requires
the confidence of a god raining
death, or no God. Idyllic beauty
brings solace to homesick men:
mountain streams, woodland belts,
wildlife exposed. Above the base,
white-capped sentinels hunch
over training flights. These monoliths
have survived shaking earth, raised
imperfection. A plane fin shimmies
like a pine bough in winter winds
or a man's navigating life's course.
Birds soar between the peaks,
the only survivors of dinosaurs
that crushed trees into stone.
Perspective is a moving target.

Line Outside Lenin's Tomb

First a wrinkled pickle of a woman lies
to you about its duration. Five minutes
in this queue would seem like a month's
march to Stalingrad. Rain is inconveniently
one degree too warm for snow. Gray-jacketed
militia order you to stop at a series of invisible
lines. You travel in packs alongside Ukrainians
with English boyfriends and a student from Fresno
who is reminded of the wait for Space Mountain.
One *chelovek* pitches to you that he will share
secrets you already know, like how the body rot
from syphilis eats even patron saints from below.
You've waited half your life to plunge into Moscow,
now halted at metal detectors and forced to check
bags where you are charged for each camera phone.
The graves surrounding Lenin have fresh-cut flowers,
including Stalin's bust, whose compatriots all appear
to be weeping from the eyes. Stony stares continue
from each guard as you descend long balustrades
into the vault. You cannot imagine softer features
on a matrushka or cleaner glass revealing moon
skin, goose hair, river suit and blood drapery.
You pause in your circuit and a soldier elbows you
to continue into the deluge with aching feet and no
map. Past metros, farmers markets, bars and banks,
you press on, leaving churches and fog in your wake.
You trudge along the river to a street that unspools

alongside barracks and soldiers on Sunday strolls.
Two by two, they pass to some unknown destination
and distant lands that bring wetness to men's boots.

Baby CPR

I am the only one alone with my rubber
doll weighted with BBs, my lifeless
baby with lips parted so I can stick
a finger down her throat to scoop out
imaginary food matter and regurgitation.
My wife is home sick in bed and I copiously
take notes. There are many ways to kill
a baby, I find, but just one way to give life.
I learned this from my father or mother,
the Sunday comics or the pink flamingos
on the lawn, the first zeppelin to go down
in flames or the unlatched bra in the back
row of the State Theater. I am the only one
alone with my life-size baby manikin.
Around me are couples, grandparents,
families taking turns blowing hard into balloon
lungs, pressing fingers below the sternum
to start the heart. All I can think about are lips:
how many of them have kissed this baby
and if this makes me a terrible father.
I am told when to hold my infant upside
down, what poisons to treat with charcoal,
and the thin cap that covers their heads
when they've been wrested from their first
watery dream. I bounce my baby nervously
on my knee. There are so many ways
to fail and too many adults still crawling
through life on scraped knees, with night

sweats, tantrums and lights on above their beds.
Hands are raised around the room, questions
asked, the eyes of mothers resting on me.
But all I can think about is what my daughter
will see first: my hands reaching out to catch
her or the shadows they'll throw as she cries
from the cold, already a traveler into the light.

Interrogator's Notebook

We learned to translate minesweeper
from Russian, read a relief map upside down,
empty a man with the least effort possible.
A soldier is an open book when the ink
is his fingertip. Sometimes even the subtle
tricks will do: waking a prisoner every few
minutes, pulling triggers of unloaded revolvers,
smiles that mimic a closing vise. We wrote
about stolen battle plans, officer predilections
and desperate meanderings. But the truth
can only be found inside men and what we do
when no can see our hate and intervene.
The interrogator's notebook is more frightening
when closed. That means the questions
have ended and another long night begins
for captured troops who warm themselves
with shadows as a roof of desert stars pierce
their eyes, a torture of unendurable beauty.

Shaman Gets Facelift After Dream

A shaman of the Kamayurá tribe dreamed
he needed a new face, so he asked
the famous plastic surgeon to stretch
his cheeks like the head of drum, to slice
away the lumps of fat under his eyes
to release the magic trapped inside.
The spiritual leader prayed to fill the limp
sack of his dreams with scalpel and anesthesia,
the way a tree trunk is felled with axe blades,
the bottoms of tribesmen floating to shore.
A half million Amazonians have followed him
in plastic surgery, their shaman unrecognizable
since he saved the famous ecologist poisoned
by a tree frog. He made the long trip to Brasília
in a canoe with no oars and watched the cleavage
and shiny faces on the streets like a deep lagoon.
We have planted much of ourselves in the ground
before the time comes to decide: burial or ash?
There is still magic trapped in the roots of trees,
and river pods beneath the ancient banks, where
young boys dive down into the dark waters
with knives and a hunger they cannot explain.

What Has My Daughter Done Now to Pablo Neruda?

Thirteen months old, with a cackle and right
hand that flaps when she shoots across
the bleached hardwood, my daughter
darts for the poetry shelf. Her favorite
is Pablo Neruda. She keeps *Navegaciones
y Regresos* behind the French doors
by the stairs, hiding there to watch
the world through glass and to caress
the cross-shaped shadows that flutter
on the walls. And to dance with poetry,
pages flapping like wings. When teething
or too tired to sleep, she places *Love Sonnets*
in the fridge as though to eat Mr. Neruda
after she masters strained peas, minced
turkey and apple sauce. She cries when
we take him away from her. She has been
known to toss *Selected Poems* in the fireplace
with glee, as though to say something
is missing so let's begin anew, or maybe
that his politics make me burn
from the inside. What is truth if it can't
be set aflame? In the living room, she stomps
on Pablo Neruda while watching basketball,
as though it were his tomb, tap dancing
on *Winter Garden*, keeping her feet aloft
from the sinking stone, night fire and loving
cold that pulse in her though him. I have not

forbidden my girl from bruising him or sailing
him like a ship at bath time to where words
and dreams fight like lizards on a cliff beach.
She buries Pablo Neruda in her sandbox
as if a dog's ham shank or a music box
trembling in a castle she molds with spit,
sand and tiny hands. Day by day, it grows
tall and leans slightly askew, with a half-
hidden smile on a bent jacket cover.

The Red Button Outside Customs at the Mexico City Airport

No wires run to it. Two guards with machine
guns make sure the button is pushed,
one per visitor. Maybe the simple stand
is meant to cause visitors to check egos
at the gate. Or else it leads to an underground
supercomputer that double checks whether
customs agents let smugglers sneak past.
Perhaps it captures fingerprints in a collage
that will appear on U.S./Mexico border walls.
Could be a photograph is snapped to be used
by secret police or tourist hawkers who meet
you by the taxi stand with it already framed.
Each time the red disk is pressed, an angel
is named Juan, laughter fills the fenced arroyo
and a star goes supernova in some distant galaxy,
protecting us from black holes, from darkness.

I Learned to Drive in a Cemetery

My stepdad said it was convenient
in case I killed us both, accelerating
too quickly in this forest of stone.
They say most accidents occur
close to home, where we've become
accustomed to the scent of flowers
and bones. We offer up one
when the other has passed.
A hardening of marrow for each
season that's gone, long-
stemmed roses on cedar and ash.
I first hit third gear on an island
where the only building is
a shooting range. The birds know
better than to nest in the eaves.
I visited there to watch the turtles,
head filled with animal puns
and the punch line of math.
I have a father and a stepdad,
the father a step ahead in leaving,
stepdad covered in cement dust.
My hometown reeks of roses and smoke.
My stepdad's parents were there,
nestled among Germans and Poles.
He'd bought graves for us all.
It is said most homes occur
close to accidents. Two fathers
as distant as molecules of air

between skin pressed in love.
Two mothers in one body:
night enveloping sun wine
in a turtle's shell. The children knew
better than to nest in the eaves.
My sisters learned to accelerate
through shrubbery and stone.
Their brother never found his turtle
on that island of bullets and ducks
with the scent of cement and wood
pulp burning from stacks. It smelled
like maple syrup in breakfasts past.
We offer up one when the other
has gone. Family burrows
in the passage of seasons.
Long-stemmed roses on mantles
of cedar and ash. My wife asks
sometimes about family and home.
I tell her we learned in a cemetery
all about sex and math: division,
subtraction, bees, birds, turtles,
ducks, I, they, flowers and bones.

Human Pyramid

In Barcelona's San Jaime Square,
human pyramids teeter skyward
in the Fiesta de La Mercè
for the patron saint of castlers.
Raised above cheering balconies,
children skitter to the apex
lighter than parents, than air.
One man treads upon another
as though in a burning nightclub
or a skyscraper without moorings.
He feels a hand cradling him
aloft, presses down his heels,
feels the crunching of bone.
When our species climbed on two
legs, the third dimension burned
a desire to look down our noses,
the penthouse view ingrained.
The Tower of Babel collapsed
in a human daisy chain,
our tongues bereft, our memories
lost. When two people mount
one another, when boys peer
under the skirts of cheerleaders,
when angelic models flutter above
our dreams on impossibly long
legs, we do not look at what
is buried below. I hold my son
Leo aloft in the prince's pose

to see his kingdom unfold
at a child's parade, a falcon's view
of his father's balding head.
A mountain of flesh proceeds
us all from father to son.
He looks at his wiggling toes
and babbles as I toss him.
Already he understands
how we will rise and fall.

Exchange

We give them food. They give
us oil. We give them a bomb
that rattles teeth from a city
away. They give us white flags
that hide revolvers. We give
them dolphins that can detect
mines three miles through murky
waters. They give us sandstorms
that are like the wrath of God.
We give them families banding
together in cities lit by candles,
listening out of shattered
windows for the desert wolf.
They give us families divided
with placards on two street
corners, traffic halted, life
filled with horns, sirens.
We give. They give more.
There is so much giving
in war, it makes you
tired from the giving.

Mine

My father taught me to fire a gun
on my grandfather's gold mine north
of Manley, Alaska—the first time I'd seen
him in twelve years. We carried rifles
for bears, for the mistrust of strangers
migrating iceward from the States.
I was accepted by the miners, the great-
grandson of a sourdough, already expert
in the yawning chasm between people
and land. My father fondled a revolver
like a man used to having his best
friend within arm's reach. At daybreak,
we mounded mud with dozers and blasted
it down a sluice with freezing river water,
gold flakes catching in wooden slots
like the unformed words we swallowed.
My father was exotic on that northern
slope, as pungent and dark as blackberry wine
passing between lovers' lips, the bottomless
sky we feel when we wake to ourselves.
At night, we gulped whiskey and slapped
mosquitoes, listening to grandpa rant about
the war that would one day engulf us all,
the sun refusing to die above the glaciers.
At dawn, we woke to a bear cub pawing
through the trash. Even I was not afraid.
My father unholstered his pistol and handed
it to me. I saw he wanted this connection

through death. Time was...just time. We were
separated by a distance no bullet to flesh
could span. I missed the shot on purpose,
the cub scampering into the underbrush.
My father stared at me in bewilderment,
then a glint of fear. We took the day off
from mining and drove dirt bikes into town,
where he introduced me as his son, the killer.

Countdown to Harmonic Convergence

10   A tall man and skinny man stand together,
     gripping their control keys, readying to fire.
9   A hobo lifts his house on a pole high above
     his head in anticipation of outrunning apocalypse.
8   Infinity has been turned sideways, dislodging
     the humans mistakenly on a pleasure ride.
7   A boomerang in ready position can turn
     on the man that wields it, scud whistling.
6   A snake swallowing its prey shows us how
     big things can disappear, even our world.
5   Is this a villain swiping at us with a hook
     or a worried director yanking us offstage?
4   This is the proverbial fork in the road,
     hand above the console, no return.
3   We shiver in night sweats as we imagine
     the breasts of every mother and lover.
2   Rockets in flight are like the flopping
     laces of a boy racing from manhood.
1   The runway is straight and unimpeded,
     reminding us of the horizon, arcing away.
0   Is this a pit, fingertip on a button, or dragon
     descending? The wheel can be reinvented.

Doors

do not touch kings. They groan
their complaints and desire wings
instead of hinges. Some dream of being
trap doors so that they can spring
darkness on their tormentors.
Others rarely feel the key's lash.
Doors can be floors, walls or even
ceilings. Some look out onto sun-
soaked lakes while others flush
in rage from the heat of hospital
incinerators. Crypts have doors, dogs
too, but open doors do not always bring
good neighbors. A few doors have smaller
doors at eye level so that the meek can
spy on those who seek to barge inside.
A few doors remember being cut
from roots and leaves, and these bang angrily
from the wind in ghost towns and along
war-torn streets. Some doors are wrapped
in human clothes and they are mostly closed.

Fashion District Accessory

What is in the bulging garbage bag
set like a hat on the head of a woman
treading downtown L.A. at lunch hour?
Not Styrofoam—wind would push it
into traffic. Empty containers of Sriracha
or salt crystals from Machu Picchu?
Perhaps sleeping kittens, lost tomes of
sensual Chinese poets, passengers from
a future moon camp, butterfly effect be
damned. It could be worn ballet slippers
hauled to garment elves or schoolbooks
for accounting night classes. Probably
not unanswered mail from a husband
trapped on an isle occupied by the Japanese
between world wars. Laundry most likely,
or every stitch she owns. Mystery stays
intact with no teeter other than my fork
on an empty salad plate. Sports statues
seem more tenuous than her straight back,
her full black sack punctuating the horizon,
the final point of a sentence about L.A.

Zen and the Art of Interrogation

An interrogator meets a one-armed man
on a bridge made of bamboo. In his dreams,
he had beaten the prisoner with the man's
own arm, asking him to explain how the wind
plotted to extinguish the sun. Or was it real?
The interrogator snaps a slat out of the cage
over the roaring waters and plays it like a flute,
shrill and savage. The man remembers the bending
notes, the raw screams, but not the interrogator.
Not anymore. He flaps his extra arm sleeve wildly.
The interrogator cackles at his beloved whirly-bird
and his foot slips through the bridge hole, causing
the spine to crack, the bones to separate as any Army
surgeon would know. The interrogator plummets,
twisting in air, turning to the light, his master,
for orders. The wind answers, exhaling a swathe
of fabric over the interrogator's eyes as he is swept
into deep waters. The sun disappears, his questions
turned inward. The interrogator claws at the cloth
blindfold, his answer arriving years too late;
the prisoner's missing arm had found his throat.

Space

No one knows what causes traffic
jams—it's true—video cameras
cannot squeeze sense from the trills
and squeals, nor can the appearance
of a bare-breasted model on a gravel
shoulder guarantee gridlock. You watch
the vendors beneath the ivied over-
pass, waiting for the inevitable Nam vet
selling mirrors with the slogan,
"See more than you ever wanted
to explain." But that doesn't keep you
from talking to yourself like a machine
pistol, sweating shrapnel, scared of what
the silence may bring. Through the sun
roof the gray curtains are poised to be
parted by an unseen hand, perhaps God
in some dire hurry. In traffic jams,
brake lights melt the dusk with bloody
eyes and a voice on the radio tells you
the traffic will be thick for miles...
as if you didn't already know how
swiftly the lonely crowds swarm and
that solitary runners slow on mountain
trails when nobody's watching.

Liar Liar

A mother in my son Leo's nursery
school claims her daughter named
herself. Absurd, unless we have
forgotten the labels of everything
no longer with us: the thing like
oatmeal but not, the flu I caught
from girls, the melancholy band
that made everyone want to kick
or kiss me. That imaginary world
with a king crab that I swore
to my kindergarten teacher lived
in the boiler room. A uniform is
a form of lie. I have asked for name,
rank, identification only to face
silence. What comes next.

Time to a Rock

His seed was slow, her womb
barren, their two terriers neutered,
their garden now just pollen
in the breeze, their home without
moorings, on an island adrift.
A rock knows more about loss
than we, growing smaller since
its birth from where the earth's
fiery pit unfolded its core and fused
with the spew of the sea.
His grief was a flower, her
impatience a fist, their two
terriers whimpering in the summer
garden filled with yellow stubble,
afraid to go beneath the porch.
The rock has known the pain
of thunderstorms, the abrasions
from boys hurling them in a battle
of vacant yard, the crush of feet,
the crackling of sunlight and air.
He left her for awhile. She hid
her grief beneath a stone. The dogs
were split, the garden under snow.
From under the porch we can see
him returning, her flowing to him.
The pebble beneath the porch

quivered in the wind, trying
to remember. Above it felt a house
creaking dangerously beneath
the weight of children's feet.

The Hangman Retires in Twenty-Nine Palms

*A piece of toast cracks
like a neck from a noose
precisely tied to avert pain,*
the hangman in retirement
mused inside his Nicaraguan
hammock, the only thing
he'd strung up since leaving
the Army behind. He'd shown
the ropes to the Iraqi soldiers
who executed Saddam on TV,
and answered only to Winston,
a cowboy's name seeped in tar,
and his penchant for lassoing
future ex-wives with death knots.
He loved staring across desert
hot springs among descendants
of World War I mustard gas
victims and mad gold miners,
scuttling lizards and experimental
windmills, Hollywood film crews
and stargazing drum troops.
He learned to read the future
napping in strangers' shadows,
conversant with lull and loss.
Death was a part of him now.
He miscounted cactus arms,

downed rattlesnake mescal,
and whistled mortar shells
on the sand dunes at dusk.
Love found him in reclusion,
a blind spa masseuse who'd
unknotted him with alias grace
and kind fury. His past tumbled
loose from his taut mouth,
his tongue testing an odd smile
like slate between his teeth.

Mapping

We can make a map with flour and milk,
dye the grass green, sculpt mountains
from cookie dough with icing for arctic
caps and ripped-up jeans for waterways,
but there is no atlas from the laughter
that comes from losing ourselves in things.
We can make a map with water and paper,
pen and sand, erect landmarks that shrivel
in wind shear and solemn vows, form ruins
with our mouths that others will refute
or spend a lifetime seeking like Spanish
galleons in the fountains of the Everglades.
We can make a map out of ceiling cracks,
use a mirror and walk backwards through
our lives, concoct a contingency plan
for when gravity will fail, so our families
will not bolt out the windows in the night
or disappear in the sky like hot air balloons.
We can make a map out of the body,
measure ridge tops and rivulets, force
tremors and tidal waves, melt glacier
streams that sink into the skin like cool
breath against the forests of the arms
or stalagmites in the recesses of the heart.
We can make a map out of selfishness,
turn people into guide posts and find short

cuts, tunnels, fault lines, lovers' lanes.
Yet there's no map for the light that blinds
us or the shadows that root beneath
our feet, the dark places we turn to home.

The Incredible Disappearing Interrogator

The interrogator loses himself one morning peering
into the mirror, each wrinkle a cache of tiny broken
things. He searches for clues how a dinosaur hunter
sweeps sand from giant femurs. He knows how to shake
foxhole dirt off his quarry, to unearth "yes" on a man's
lips when the sky is on fire. The world may very well
end while he sifts through the broken hourglass
of prisoners buried to their necks. He'd searched
for happiness as a boy in hidden places. His first "?"
was the curve of a belt against his spine as his father
interrogated him about the devil within. He hid toys
in the sandbox by the garage, entombing army
men and candy supplies. He pretended to care
about his father tinkering, teeth clamped on smoke.
There is sand that even tears will not wash away
through the years. It remains in your body hair,
each granule a message inscribed by fingernails
into flesh. The sandbox later becomes a grave
as the interrogator buries his father, felled
by cancer. The final dirt packing the coffin
he shakes from his scalp and presses beneath
his boot. The interrogator looks in the mirror
each anniversary and sees his father there.
The traffic outside his window reminds
him of surf, the way men drown on men.

Daytrippers

You knew them in the crib,
the ones who stared through
the slats like prison bars.
The ones quick to cry,
to babble, to crawl straight
for swimming pools, street
curbs and drain cleaner
when you turned your back.
In grade school, you knew
them by their shadows seated
in the back row, one eye
at the window, sun burning
through them onto the chalk
board, casting doubt on long
division and the need for cursive.
In high school, you knew them
by their absence: empty desk,
lockers swollen with unopened
books, cigarette stains on jeans,
rings beneath their eyes, cars parked
in woods with cheap wine and loud
music. In college, you wanted to go
to their parties with neon lights,
blood-colored punch and speakers
faced out the windows. You knew
their cars for the caked dust, worn

tires and peeling decals, their long
departure from us already in motion.
When you think of them now,
they are like clouds on the horizon:
storm brewing, dormant keepers of snow
caps, jagged light and thunder claps
that shiver deliciously, the risks
we take that make us shake in fear,
the rain that wakes us slowly.

Bronzing of the Boots

When they blew up the dictator's
statue, marble sword and stallion
raining on the streets, I winced,
even as soldiers spat on the rubble
for cameras, for the mighty fallen.
Atlas was all our fathers, right?
You know him. He'd rather break
than drop a hint. And break he did,
his statue crumbling on some distant,
immeasurable shore. In war, the world
rolls behind us, unbearable, on our heels.
It is a child's marble, a random boulder.
Some nights, we can barely see it beneath
us, hidden like testicles, sure to disappear.
Some mornings we watch an irresistible
ball of blue that could either be ocean,
sky or God's own eye. In Baghdad,
soldiers have left their boots behind,
littering the street in growing mounds
taking shapes like the silhouettes of men
who do not mind picking stone from feet.

Somnambulist

First to become restless, your fingers
wander the shadowy corridors, fumble
over first edition books and blouses, close
over hidden objects as heavy as the world.
Your mouth inhales the clouds like pastry:
cumulus, stratus, nimbus, a confectioner's
fantasy life unfurled. Your tongue writhes,
blistered by some remembered pain.
Ears take flight into forest glades,
in perfect pitch with ladybugs and pincher
bugs, sinkholes sucking ferns into the depths,
the thin dry snap of leaf and twig.
Your feet float in a tub of tingling water
and rose petals. When the heat rises
to steam, they are rubbed in ice by hands made
quick by the fickleness of books and blouses.
Eyes wander into dark, smoky rooms,
intoxicated by undulating brown waves
and the flirtation of mirrors. You like being
seen in the ricochet of time moving backwards.
Sometimes your senses are nervous fish darting
through your dream. They throw themselves
over waterfalls onto your sheets, reforming
into the perfect you, a monster, the only you.

Brain Bruise

A woman in my office smacked
her forehead so hard against the divide
between her cubicle and her neighbor's
that she felt a pain in the back
of her head for days. The emergency
room doctor told her that the injury
was really her brain colliding against
her skull, the impact a catalyst
to CAT scans and dizzying vertigo.
History is filled with brain bruise,
invading armies marauding on shores
that will one day vanquish them.
Hitler once held a puppy longingly
while London blazed inconsolably,
a damp rag soaking Gandhi's brow,
hiding radiation blisters on Japanese
faces. Monsters grow from men's
fertile imagination for destruction.
When two plates grind underground
the quake resonates on faraway lines.
Two people collide on a subway meeting
decades before their future children drift
apart in old age. Our skulls are soft
as we grow into beings hard enough
to cause, to create, to crash hard. My heart
some days feels gushingly gone; my gait
reverts to marching as all ex-soldiers do
when headaches crack the world's casing.

Into the White

We called it white lightning when we could
get it, crystal when we could not. It turned
bright lights into winking eyes and tinged
the night in sharp white delineations
like freshly-poured chalk on a baseball
infield. We breathed white hope and told
white lies, but only to ourselves. Others
got beaming white teeth, the white flag
of surrender and white-knuckled fists.
We draped ourselves in white like snow
on frantic playgrounds so many years
before until we were ghosts, a fountain
of fractured light in rearview
mirrors, a white bronco doomed
to wander the earth. Even when
we refused to go into the white,
it filled our insides like a circus
performer who swallows
a light bulb and stands
in the rain for hours
on end, waiting...
for lightning
to strike.

The Interrogator and Priest

As close as brothers, altar boys at Saint
Francis, dipping pocket combs in holy
water, debonair in velvet sashes and dark
socks. They loved the zany prestidigitation
of Jesus, the limp arms welcoming them
to their future, closed eyes projecting
fervent anguish, twisted love. Each boy
chose a path of righteous indignation.
The interrogator's pistol, on his hip,
was worn like a cross for his prisoners,
promising absolution or jagged wrath.
The priest's confessional, a holding cell,
reminiscent of a dimly lit boy's bedroom,
probed parishioners' secrets, exculpated
sinners from bombed villages, strafed whores.
Dunking a man's head beneath the water
was soothsaying to the interrogator, baptism
to the priest swigging wine to electro trance.
Bawdy texts twittered between the brothers
on their travels to turn men into brethren;
they shared recipes for goat stew, onion
dip, skin rolls pinched to make a point.
They each agreed that the other would ask
God one question when the time arrived,
and they were certain the answer would be
the same, their long-forgotten family name.

Dictator

My daughter India is a country.
Our borders collapse as she barrels
into my knees at battle speed,
or invades my dreams with night
cries and the wonder of what
can be. When she is sick, I wage
war with a compress and chemicals
to the body, wiping out the ill.
When she erupts and hits my flank,
I count to ten, the time a bomb's
whistle separates an explosion.
What will her country be?
She orders me around and I
laughingly call her my 37-inch
dictator. I am as powerful
and helpless as America
floundering with fatherhood,
with unflinching convictions.
Here's the fear we won't admit:
our children will surpass us
and we will fade, but how will
we spend our hours as tottering
steps accelerate to moon rockets,
and who we are is what we do.
We can clench our fists and stomp
our feet when feel lost inside,
or spread hands under small cheeks,

big eyes. The best soldiers can read
a map with their fingers. A father
has more skill as he navigates river
tears and gully smiles. He traverses
bumps and bruises without stumble,
his eyes closed in a lullaby march,
using a map with no borders but air.

The Moscow Metro

Strangers press like fish in tins. Pale skin
nestles in dark jackets, knee flesh peeking
above slush-stained boots, fur-liners and face
masks flashing in shadowy cubbies. The scale
makes me miniature alongside craggy statues
of poets and madmen, escalators boring into earth
on endless tracks, edged with gang writing on dusty
ledges. In winter, the doors from the outside swing
like a hammer, heavy and fast. There are *pirozhki*
with hidden bones, chain-smoking women buying
lingerie underground, soldiers cradling flowers,
kiosks of concert performances, teenagers
on guitars next to *babushkas* with prayer rugs,
windowless internet cafes, the smell of urine
and life well lived. My love for you is like this.

Whale Holes and Belly Buttons

My neighbor vacuumed his lawn,
a tattoo of a dragon on his forearm,
a tea-towel tied to his waist,
begonias shimmying at the blowhole.
He vacuumed to clean dewdrops
from the rye stalks and petal camisoles.
He vacuumed full-skirted lavender
and snails retreating into shells.
He vacuumed rose hips when hungry
and grass backs when his loneliness
drew him into the darkness for a smoke
to stare at his wife's yellow garden.
He vacuumed because she told him
she'd return the day he regained control
but there was nothing he could do
to eradicate the swear words and car
exhaust, let alone her fearful sobs
that he would one day suck her whole.
He vacuumed chestnut husks in roof gutters
and nursery rhymes over the hedgerows,
imagining the children that might have been,
the hexagon light in his cigarette end.

Namesake

My grandfather's twin was named Adolf,
card hawk and husky breeder, interred
at the end of World War II, the wrong
time to get caught holding five aces.
An Italian political party offered to pay
parents to name their child after Benito
Mussolini or his wife Rachele, to keep
their names alive in Rome. If we could
name all towns and signposts, we would
pass on the shape of our lovers' lips,
raised eyebrow, anger bumps on skulls
in a tortured cartography. There is no
difference when deciphering a bumper
sticker, T-shirt or tomb a thousand years
from now. Names wear us devotedly,
until the end, no real answers given.

Perishables

One summer my family went
rooting through the woods for beer
cans, searching though patches
of ferns and campfire remains
for bleached carcasses of grain.
The best hunting was behind
the cement plant where we
would fill our plastic bags
and dip our toes in brown
water, joking how the trout
might confuse them for worms
which we gathered for bait,
those carcasses of earth.
We were always searching
for something—my parents
for huckleberries large as eye-
balls, my sisters for men
to take them away. I'm not
sure I knew enough to look
anything but surprised at a trout
gasping in air, a beer can shot
from target practice, a worm
split on the end of a hook,
each half falling home to earth,
divided, but insistent—family.

Different Kinds of Fire

Marshmallow roast, ignition flint,
red-tongued leviathan hotel blaze.
Imprint of cookie sheet, tattoo
of candle wax. Lover sizzling
in someone's sure hands. Once,
I helped smother a forest fire
with a green poncho after night
range, my fellow soldiers beating
the trees like in bayonet practice.
We were told when seeking cover
to take two steps for parachute flare,
and one for nuclear bomb, enough
time to fling yourself in the nearest
depression, eyes shut, winter fire.

Norman Rockwell's 'Mother Spanking Her Child'

More interesting than the scorching
consternation dimpling her brow
or the hardback tome on child
psychology in her lap or the ivory hair
brush warmed to the task at hand
are the shards of household goods
scattered beneath her dining room
chair. A hammer lies beside a shattered
vase, a hand-mirror jagged and leaking
luck, the uncoiled guts of a red alarm
clock. Did the boy take the hammer
from his father's tool drawer and wade
away with timber flying at what fueled
his mother's vanity: the 4:30 a.m. mask
of cream and face memorized like state
capitals, or did she herself smash them
in anger? The vase—one hit was
enough on its backside, the mirror
slightly more, seven, eight, nine, the alarm
obliterated into tailbone, twelve o'clock,
the hammer no good for the bruises
it would make. The boy is reddening
in her hands, his face hidden, his reflection
underfoot. On the cover of *The Saturday
Evening Post*, it is November 23, 1933—

the Depression not yet an uncomfortable
memory. In the ensuing war of strong
and weak, how come we did not see
her stilettos cast shadows on the carnage?

The Alchemy of Daybreak

There are an uneven number of nights.
I am a monk chanting at the moon.
The day of the week escapes me
because of ten days that never happened in 1582.
I am a monk chanting at the moon,
Gregorian calendar folded in my lap
because of ten days that never happened in 1582.
A deer dances on a raindrop, in the rafters.
Gregorian calendar folded in my lap,
wind chimes drown the blare of traffic.
A deer dances on a raindrop, in the rafters.
There is a 50 gallon drum of water in the basement.
Wind chimes drown the blare of traffic.
An Army pal emails me from the Book of Numbers.
There is a 50 gallon drum of water in the basement.
If it is Thursday, I have missed another appointment.
An Army pal emails me from the Book of Numbers.
I wonder if my body will store beer like a camel's.
If it is Thursday, I have missed another appointment.
The sun wears a bonnet made of glass.
I wonder if my body will store beer like a camel's.
Lightning bursts over the beaches of Dover.
The sun wears a bonnet made of glass.
I am looking for you where the day breaks.
Lightning bursts over the beaches of Dover
because of ten days that never happened in 1582.
There are an uneven number of nights.
I am looking for you where the day breaks.

Captive

These layoff days lead you to a windowless
room and a cardboard box handed to you.
The truth is that you are not wanted
by everyone you wish to impress.
The room transforms into a white house
left by a father or mother, dusty trophy,
childhood home sold, the lover who left
a hole that you patched with fistfuls of dirt.
You ask yourself if you are worthy
and the pain you feel is more real
than a glib answer, glass half-tanked,
hope passed to children that could be
lies, could be your way of forgetting.
Truth is not found by the glow of night
light or rescuers' search beams, bare
bulb of the inquisitor or candlelit bath.
This day, this cardboard box you carry,
these dangling things are not you.

The Impatient Poet

Start with suicide.
Gather jacket blurbs from the bearded
canon. Italicize your ghost voice
and impress critics at seances.
Exercise the thin poem from the fat
one. Starve it from adverbial carbs
and blow a whistle during calisthenics.
Inject animal spirits into your verse,
and scare readers to hide in your pages.
Be experimental. Scrawl your visions
on eggs and mark fragile to publishers
with a poetry expiration date.
Make every line an epiphany
of war, sex, death and MFA malaise.
Clone drunken and celibate versions
of yourself to keep your mojo humming.
Obsess about children and death,
because they veer too closely
in bent pages and tattered ambition.
It's the poem that writes you.

Things I've Left Behind

An M-16 carbine, oiled and passed to the next grunt,
muscle memory such that years later I could still
disassemble in the dark more easily than unhooking
a bra. A plastic bucket of Army men in my mother's
attic, plastic edges worn from hardwood missions,
mixed with cowboys, Indians, strange battles looming.
8 mm footage from my college kung fu epic, filmed
in Russian. A '69 Chevelle abandoned five miles
from the airport, bayonet and peyote tossed into brush.
My dog tags dangle on the bedpost of a woman
who led me into former Yugoslavia. The necktie
from my first formal dance flung to lariat a falling
star, my best friend plummeting from Jack Daniels.
The ear clip from those lost years in New Orleans
among men in trench coats and women in Egyptian
jewelry. The bag of pot I buried at the Canadian
border with Woody, the felled hair, skin window
to sun, rain, pitiless drones strafing battlefields
won and lost. Anger, pride, these things take
longer, flotsam of fights with women, tests
with men, so much pain and glory over days
that broke skin, hearts and bridges. On this path
still half-traveled, I keep fused bones, shadow
seeds, love of children in a place that even
strangers can see, these steps, this passage of me.

Lessons

I remember the morning
you asked me: do plants have
bones, do eyeglasses have bones,
do presidents, television actors
and parakeets have bones?
Do earthquakes miss their
bones? Do bones have bones?
I remember the afternoon
you asked me: do sunsets have
questions, annoying questions
that linger in glimmering shades
of marmalade and raspberries,
questions that burn, that titillate,
that scare us like the dark
hours between sun and moon,
questions about whether roosters
peck each other to death while
their hens cluck at day's end?
I remember the evening
you asked me about where
I was going, my underwear
drawer, the folds of my wallet,
the bulges in my clothes,
the smells of my body,
the plants that have withered
boneless and alone, birds
of every song disappearing
into the horizon with secret

lives and red-drenched wings.
And we both remember the night
you asked about love and death,
and I told you they're a real pain
in the ass when they roost outside
your window. I explained how
nightingales mimic the calls
of other birds to flutter close,
to steal their eggs, like adults
who've learned all the answers,
with no songs to call their own.

City of Braille

I stagger, raise the sash and undress
her masquerade—the curves, the smells,
green cups of meadowland breathing
life into the fist of concrete melodies.
I know this city like the back of my hand,
but the back of my hand has no name,
not like palm, thumb or knuckling
streets. And what about those freckles
that fade and spark with smog and sun,
or memories that tread the cityscape
like cirrus fingers kneading braille?
Some cities have teeth like wolves,
others a gaping maw that makes us
yearn for what we have destroyed.
White fire rises from the caverns
blinding us in grief and a lover's rage.
From the rubble, we ache to touch
the sky even as we bar our windows
and bolt our gates. And yet the unnamed
known hovers just beyond our reach:
the off-key symphony of subway
brakes, a waving hand that guides
you into the blessed turn lane, slick
shoulders on an asphalt court at sun-
down. I dream this city so well I call
her she, but how can I gauge the sex
of the skyline any better than I can

my desire for bustle or the spittle
swapped between strangers in a curio
shop as they stare at each other's
coffee mugs and whisper, "New York,
Los Angeles, Baton Rouge, Kalamazoo,
I love you, who are you, I love you."

Ghost Stand

Two eagles nest in a bleached stand
of dead pines, preserved in brine
from the earthquake that dropped
their roots thirty feet into ocean.
Tidewater glaciers ripple onto ice
fields that yawn hundreds of miles,
the crackle of ice plummeting
like thunder, like eggs breaking.
If one hatchling were to be destroyed
in the shell, the couple might try
again. Across the channel, a stone
fort points six-inch guns down
to repel the Japanese. In Seward,
tsunami signs point up the mountain,
the town crisped from when oil tanks
poured a river of flames from giant
waves, the next earthquake inevitable,
the next war unbearably close,
ice fields disappearing into dusk,
two eagles living among the ghosts.

Requiem for Pluto

A small black orb is watching you
untraceable by the human eye.
Sometimes you feel there is a pinhole
boring through the sloping neck top,
exposing the frontal lobe to scrutiny.
You imagine the all-seeing gaze
of a dark-star deity guiding you.
You look for it from your favorite
coffee shop, staring at the same
street corner for a woman's dress
to rise, drawn by gravity that should
not be. The day you saw him appear
through the bottom of your water
glass no one believed you found
the God of the Underworld strolling
your neighborhood but you had faith
in the power of things unseen.
Your waitress listens to your dreams
and dots your check with a circle.
You imagine a smiling face there
waiting to be eternally discovered.

The Lie of the Land

It began as a joke, with legions of dolts
and light bulbs, historical figures in bars,
doors locked to knock-knocks,
the kidding of lovers, imbedded thorns.
It slithered beneath the surface,
dead-language calligraphy on X-rays,
the swell of flesh in faded denim,
bullets inserted in oiled chambers,
an aperture yawning in your sidewalk
you fear will swallow squirrels, the sun.
It lengthens in shadows on leap years,
reunion dances, convention flirtations,
inauguration speeches and the gummy
legs of racing foals fusing into form.
It exists because you ignore its desire
until there is no reason to believe
in corner offices and planted moon
flags, neighbors who've fled and bled.
The skin of the world puckers,
and the sky ripples from our needs,
missile silos and infidels in night shirts,
interrogators washing windpipes, salon style.

When Buildings Fall

There are some things we cannot catch:
a single strand from our scalp, threading
air like an acorn gyroplane as we fumble
for it, a mosquito fish suddenly plopping
onto shore. Or a palm crab clacking
down the steps of the United Nations,
security teams in pursuit as rivets
cascade from the gusset seaming
New York, snow-ash disappearing.
We wrap ourselves in bombazine and hope
our tears bridge the spark gap between
life and the spavin we bear from below.
At night, my lover holds onto my tussock
and our lovemaking screams detente
like birch trees on newly paved Volgograd
or antiparticles meeting on a dusky Paris
boulevard. Last earthquake, my neighbor's
Warhol fell from its perch. She said between
it and that claptrap Faulkner, it's lucky
she wasn't maimed…like we all are
from what we cannot catch, be it planes
aimed straight at our windows, jaws
collapsing like molten steel girders
or bodies thrown at us from the sky.

Upon Hearing 56 Miles of the L.A. River Will Become a State Park

The river cleaves us,
it brings us two shores.
Snoozing smog,
moon-blooming jasmine.
Green water,
brown water.
Egrets, airplanes.
On an atoll a man sits
cross-legged, wearing
a plastic bag
as a hat, meditating
to the cars grazing overhead.
Largemouth and catfish
are showing on hooks.
A little bit of everything,
but not a lot of anything.
The river leaves us,
it darts through our veins.
Jacaranda,
coffee table.
Burning bush,
fragrant weed.
We are Hercules bending
mountain streams
in our fists,
a child bending
over sidewalk to learn

the language of roots.
Try crawdads and waterdogs
for bass, PowerBait
for trout and search
the high lakes for bluegill.
The river has forgotten
its way to the sea.
You can stare at a man
in a plastic hat
for hours
and still not see
the same waters twice.
Our children bring the river
to school in a box.
A dripping faucet
frightens us awake
late at night.
Nightcrawlers are working
best. Bass are biting
on spinner baits and plastic
worms. Some redear perch.
The river wishes it had
no bottom but man.
Drowning in air,
breathing sea salt.
Casting a net,
capturing ourselves.
Staring up through placenta
we see God.
Examining our children,

the death of the river
can't be far behind.
Fly fishermen are using nymphs.
Catfish are so-so.
Bluefish are starting
to show at the cattails.
The river is naked.
We hum its song in the night.
Grass rises,
concrete recedes.
Fish feed
in our untested depths.
Two banks are connected
by a park bridge.
What man will we find
there on the atoll?
Pack up tackle and bait,
wash knives at the shore.
A slight rain is forecast.
Look into the depths.
The river cleaves us,
the river leaves us.
The river has forgotten,
the river wishes.
The river is naked.
It brings us two shores,
it darts through our veins.
It makes its way to the sea
with no bottom but man.
We hum its song in the night.

The Interrogator's Fishing Tale

When the interrogator was just becoming a man,
he believed himself to be a fisherman. He baited
his hook with promises and clever turns of phrase,
and cast it into an ocean he did not know. He saw
shapes twist along in the current and found himself
aroused by the glinting wave caps. He wanted truth
to swim. After the interrogator was educated for war,
ocean was a cup he learned to offer a thirsty prisoner.
His early questions were expunged. He clamped
his lips to capture the fire and expelled a cigarette
cloud into the raining eyes of another. He turned
to his mirror and practiced his smirk disappearing
like POWs behind black walls. He imagined
the women he'd ply outside the fort and asked
his smoky reflection for the truth or else.
When the interrogator mastered his art, he was
more shark than fisherman. He rushed toward light
from unsleeping depths. He nibbled off a foot,
an eyebrow, a nip of skin from neck nape, just
enough to satisfy his urge to swallow his prey
whole. Later, his wife held him as he rolled
in his sleep. He asked for only as much truth
as he needed. Near the end of his career,
the interrogator mulled the chum on hooks
with no possibility of catch or release.
In the surf of St. Thomas, he had placed
two gutted snappers on the feet of a Cuban
refugee, blood and guts staining the water

with a briny confession. The rueful interrogator
listed sharks that would devour men: great white,
tiger, bull, and then promised he would add
a bearded prison not yelping out answers.
The interrogator could not wear leather slippers
without thinking about the thick skin dragging
on the floor. The truth was a shade of red.
When the interrogator grew long in the tooth,
he felt the ocean roil in his stomach, fish made
captive and placed on ice when he embraced
his wife and sons. He asked nothing of his
family, afraid to bare his third row of teeth.
They wanted the truth to wriggle out of him.

India Ivy

With my daughter India nestled
in a front pack on my chest, I feel
almost beautiful. Men nod appreciatively.
Women beam, poking at the belly
on my belly, tiny arms and feet flailing,
men calling her a doll, a wind-up
toy, women telling me she is fidgety
and alert. On our walks, I point out
things to her. *This is a mushroom,
it is beautiful, tasty in salads.
It is deadly, growing in shadows.*
I wonder if she will hate her name.
India Ivy—a hopeless romantic?
Or a nymph who will travel
from man to man, country
to country. Will she be invaded
by soldiers or overwhelmed
by brick and iron latticework?
When I walk with her on my belly,
people coo and reach for her
as though trying to remember
a language they spoke as kids:
Polish, Spanish, Cajun, Cherokee.
They've forgotten what it is
to be. *This is a firefly, I say.
It is luminescent, an insect
to be crushed. It is nocturnal
like the moon. Without its wings*

*it shimmers like Christmas lights,
like disco balls.* She dances on my
chest, giggling to make people
turn their heads and smile
at her. She is a flirt, a country.
She is a weed. Her borders are
at risk; she is in bloom. I wonder
what I will do to the first boy
who looks at her with lust?
Here's my dirty secret: I joke
to friends that she will be
a basketball player by day,
exotic dancer by night.
*This is an ant. It is insignificant,
it is a horde. They crawl through
my dreams. Keep away from them.
They will nibble where you cannot
see. Dripping with honey, they
will eat your soul, these tiny
men.* You are a revolution,
a jump rope rhyme. I worry
your head will hit the concrete
like an egg. *This is a chicken
omelet, mother and daughter
as one.* You are a nation
of tendrils, pouring from me
like wine. I'm afraid of being
afraid for you. *This is a poem*

that I've written for you.
It's a lie—it's the truth.
This causes you to cry
from hunger, from teething,
from missing your mother,
from tiredness. You are tears
drifting to sleep. With you strapped
to me, I feel almost beautiful.

Colophon

The body type of *Captive* is set in Sabon, created by the German designer Jan Tschichold. An influential figure in the avant-garde, Tschichold turned in his late typography to the print tradition—and its emphasis on proportion and legibility—deriving Sabon (circa 1967) from the eponymous 16th century typeface of Claude Garamond. Poem titles are Caslon 3, a slightly bolder turn-of-the-last-century version of the well-known Caslon, which dates to the 1720s and is widely considered the first type designed specifically for English. Cover and front matter titles are Tungsten, a contemporary sans serif rooted in early modern modular type by Hoefler & Frere-Jones. Their stated aim in creating this font family was a typeface forceful but not overbearing, one "more Steve McQueen than Steven Seagal," a "whiskey highball, not a martini."

www.ingramcontent.com/pod-product-compliance
Lightning Source LLC
LaVergne TN
LVHW041343080426
835512LV00006B/597